BUSTA RHYME

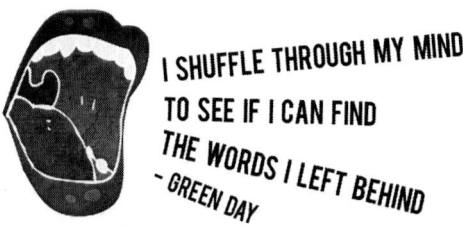

I SHUFFLE THROUGH MY MIND
TO SEE IF I CAN FIND
THE WORDS I LEFT BEHIND
- GREEN DAY

SOUTH WEST POETS

Edited By Emily Wilson

First published in Great Britain in 2017 by:

Young Writers
Remus House
Coltsfoot Drive
Peterborough
PE2 9BF
Telephone: 01733 890066
Website: www.youngwriters.co.uk

All Rights Reserved
Book Design by Spencer Hart
© Copyright Contributors 2017
SB ISBN 978-1-78820-397-5
Printed and bound in the UK by BookPrintingUK
Website: www.bookprintinguk.com
YB0333D

FOREWORD

Welcome Reader,

For Young Writers' latest competition, *Busta Rhyme*, we challenged secondary school pupils to take inspiration from the world around them, whether from the news, their own lives or even songs, and write a poem on any subject of their choice. They rose to the challenge magnificently, with young writers up and down the country displaying their poetic flair.

We chose poems for publication based on style, expression, imagination and technical skill. The result is this entertaining collection full of diverse and imaginative poetry which covers a variety of topics - from favourite sports to more serious subjects such as bullying and war. Using poetry as their tool, the young writers have taken this opportunity to express their thoughts and feelings through verse. This anthology is also a delightful keepsake to look back on in years to come.

Here at Young Writers our aim is to encourage creativity in the next generation and to inspire a love of the written word, so it's great to get such an amazing response, with some absolutely fantastic poems. I'd like to congratulate all the young poets in *Busta Rhyme - South West Poets*. I hope this inspires them to continue with their creative writing.

Emily Wilson

CONTENTS

Independent Entries

Ben Bluett (13)	1

All Saints CE School, Wyke Regis

Nataya James (12)	2
Kaitlyn Knight (11)	4
Maya Yates (12)	6
Megan Dennis (12)	7
Zak Ormes (12)	8
Lucy Heskins (12)	10
Harry Bernard Mynes (12), Lewis & Charlie Rowe (12)	11
Alfie Stokes (12)	12
Bronte Elena Greta Oliver (12) & Mya	13
Calvin Hawkins (12)	14

Brannel School, St Stephen

Bethany Gribble (12)	15
Amy Bristow (13)	16
Courtney Hitchens (13)	18
Hollie Swallow (13)	19
Summer Wade (13)	20
Olivia Ralph (13)	22
Tilly Ashby (13)	23
Alisiana Oliver (13)	24
Rhys Vandermerwe (13)	25
Chelsi Down (13)	26
Bradley Way (12)	27
Danny Oliver (13)	28
Liam Phillips (13)	29
Aaron Williams (12)	30
Charleanne Ede (13)	31
Lauren Williams (13)	32

Sarah Guy (13)	33
Billy Turpin-Brooks (13)	34
Harry Lewis (13)	35
Joshua Osborne (13)	36
Ben Millar (13)	37
Charlie Rowe (12)	38
Leah Jean Grist (13)	39
Jessica Weighill (13)	40
Cody Dalby (13)	41
Stewart Bryan Heaton (13)	42
Thomas Follington (13)	43

Clayesmore School, Blandford Forum

Ben Chick	44

Cranbrook Education Campus, Cranbrook

Dylan Green (12), Reece Dowd (11) & Harvey Levy (11)	45
Corbin (12) & Noah Homewood (12)	46

Fairfield High School, Horfield

Deborah Omolegan-Obe (13)	47
Maisie Woods	49

Hele's School, Plympton

Bethany Skelton (13)	51
Ambher Davy (15)	52
Caitlin Barnes (14)	54

Helston Community College, Helston

Cerys Siobharn Read (14)	56

Marine Academy, St Budeaux

Erin-May McMichael (13)	57
Leah Gotham (14)	58
Milly Lecount (13)	59
Jade Thomas (13)	60

Penryn College, Penryn

Eloise Beattie (15)	61
Daisy Booker (15)	62
Lila Mae Sefi (12)	64

Redruth School, Redruth

Katie Machin	66
Shaun Thomas Goodman (12)	68
Amelia Worden (12)	70
Jamie Lowenna Collick (12)	71
Leo Vaughan (12)	72
Darcey Christine Jago (12)	74
Rebekah Pearce (13)	76
Josh Ebling	78
Madison Symons	80
Kalya Christine Manley (13)	82
Adam Richards (12)	84
Kimberley Thomas (13)	85
Maisie Cornish (12)	86
Tom Clarke Sharples (12)	87
Lilli Wright	88
Deanna Watson (13)	90
Holly Thompson (12)	92
Samuel Linthwaite (13)	93
Jessica Reynolds (12)	94
Jake Neville (12)	96
Caitlin Kira Roberts (14)	97
Ben Grimsted	98
Molly-Victoria Harris (12)	99
Harley Matthews (14)	100
Eleanor Dennis (12)	101

Kacey Barber (13)	102
Emily Jose (12)	103
India Bennett-O'Brien	104
Billy Packenas (13)	105
James Glasspool	106
Curtis Holland (14)	107
Louie Fowler-Beaton	108
Joshua Weller (13)	109
Tara Charlotte Bawden (12)	110
Lilly-Rose Kelly Stannard (12)	111
Caitlyn Harris	112
Lucy Gemma Hulme (14)	113
Alfie Jack Rahn (11)	114
Mia Jose (13)	115
Gemma Richards	116
Connor Taplin (12)	117
Sophie Eddy (11)	118
Kai Jenkin (12)	119
Lewis Thomas (13)	120
Shania Medlyn	121
Thomas Lee Hocking (12)	122
Rozie Hamilton (12)	123
Trinity Sinkins (12)	124

Sidmouth College, Sidmouth

Sinead Taylor (12)	125

Stoke Damerel Community College, Stoke

Edie Mai Spooner (12)	126
Natalie Maynard (11)	127
Israel Bond (12)	128
Shania Scott (12)	129

Tavistock College, Tavistock

Joe Dix (13)	130
Douglas Radcliffe	131
Will Greep (14)	132

The Ridgeway School & Sixth Form College, Wroughton

Levi Farrow (14)	133
Hollie Zaccaro (14)	134
Eleanor Woods (14)	136
Lucy Cowell (14)	138
Patricia Caroline Carvalho (13)	140
Faith Enotse Ukpoju (14)	142
Tom Bryan Stokes (14)	144
Shannon Louise Wolton (14)	146
George Tweedale (14)	148

THE POEMS

Terrorism

Terrorism
Terrorism is happening around us
Terrorism is killing us.
Terrorism will not stop us.
I am sitting now hearing about a mindless attack.
Time will not go back,
It does not make sense.
The attack was horrifying
It is terrifying.
They will not stop us - we will win.

Ben Bluett (13)

Forget About Them, They Will Not Win

Yes, she is from a different place and yes,
She is very different from us,
But that doesn't mean you have to bully her.
Every day the bullies would come,
Every day she would run.
She would always say in her head to forget about it
Because they won't win.

You always bully her,
Just because she's a different race to you,
You treat her differently, but she would abide by the same laws.
You treat her like she's nothing,
Just a crumb on the floor,
But she's more than that, just wait, you'll see.

Does it matter she's a different race?
Does it matter she's from a different place?
She says to herself get your head in the game,
She says just forget about it, forget about them,
They won't win.

So what, she's different,
We are all different from our heads to our toes,
From our friends to our foes,
Or the shoes we all wear like Nike,
We are all different, but she is more.

Stop. No need to be a bully.
Stop. Let's be friends -
Friends until the end.
She had the courage,
The courage to be friends -
With the person bullying her.

Nataya James (12)
All Saints CE School, Wyke Regis

Fighting Cancer

This is my story about when my dad had cancer.
This is where my story began:

I remember the day
That the ambulance arrived,
Wheelchair at the ready,
They got him downstairs
And into the ambulance,
My mum in the ambulance with him
Going to Weldmar Hospice.
I went with my auntie to the hospice.

Me and my sister
Drew pictures and laid them in his coffin.
Now we keep a box filled with memories
We had together.
I had a few days off school
And spent them with my auntie.

Soon my dad passed away.
At my dad's funeral,
My sister had written a poem -
She was too sad to read it,
So the vicar read it.

We sprinkled his ashes
Into the sea
At Castle Cove beach, Weymouth.

This is my story
About when my dad had cancer.

Kaitlyn Knight (11)
All Saints CE School, Wyke Regis

Shards

I don't know what I am.

For as long as I can remember,
I have been desperately searching.

Through the shattered remains of my forgotten memories and dreams,
I pondered.

Who am I?

Each shard is just the same as the other.
The bright, uplifting glow of the colour that was once there,
Dulled by the unmerciful touch of trauma and hatred.

They lie there, unmoving, cold with regret.
This isn't who I am. Or, that was what I thought.

There it is, amongst the billowing darkness of the unwanted shards,
One, only one shard hopefully glimmers in a shade of yellow,
Similar to that of a buttercup soaked in the saturating rays of the sun.

In my cold, pale hands, now turning purple,
I cup the glowing shard welcomingly in my palms.

Maya Yates (12)
All Saints CE School, Wyke Regis

Running

Nervous, like a curled-up cobra
Adrenaline pumping throughout my body
Like a plane lined up, all set for take-off
Roller coaster of emotions

Mud splashed up my whirring legs
Can't breathe, can't stop, must keep on going
Sweat trickling down me like a spring
Sun burns upon my soaking face

The three kilometre marker, two to go
The four kilometre marker, just one remains
At last the finish line is in sight
Elated and exuberant, that is what I feel.

Megan Dennis (12)
All Saints CE School, Wyke Regis

War Hammer

The stench of rotting bodies,
Filled with bullets.
Seeing his best friends,
Surrounded, executed
One by one,
He hears yells - help - argh!

The remaining warriors of the fight,
Gather together, thinking of
A strategy to get out alive.
There were only twenty-seven of us
Remaining.
We were joined by traitors,
The enemy,
We smelt the burnt iron
Of their armour.

Suddenly, bullets hit our bodies,
Wounding us,
But not killing us... yet.
We fight on,
We shot the general
Square in the head!
Then the change,
Turning stiff,
Limb by limb.

We turn to plastic,
Picked up
And placed
In a soft box.

Zak Ormes (12)
All Saints CE School, Wyke Regis

Racism

It doesn't matter if you're black or white,
The pain is in my heart when I sleep at night.
Racism is not right.

Getting pushed into the dark alley by the bullies,
They get out a knife and jab it into my thigh,
Not knowing if I am going to die!

Scared of the terrifying days at school,
I didn't fit in because of the colour of my skin,
Hiding from the light because of my battered and bruised body.

Lucy Heskins (12)
All Saints CE School, Wyke Regis

School

All this school
Nonsense
Is hard.
Some of it bad, some of it good...
Flipping tables like you're in the hood.
Shouting at us, shouting at me
Half the time it's not even me.
Why don't you go back outside,
Flip another table, flip another lie.
All you say is just lies
Throwing a tantrum, face going red.
No more homework, no more detentions
We just want to be mentioned.

Harry Bernard Mynes (12), Lewis & Charlie Rowe (12)
All Saints CE School, Wyke Regis

Vandalism

Vandalism is a bit of litter.
Vandalism isn't using Twitter.

Vandalism is taking someone's fence,
Not using your common sense.

Vandalism is more destruction
Than it is construction.

Vandalism is drawing on walls
Not playing catch with a ball.

Vandalism is using paint to ruin cars.
Vandalism isn't going to Mars.

Alfie Stokes (12)
All Saints CE School, Wyke Regis

Noticed

Everyone is the same
Aren't they?
You just never noticed that,
You never notice love,
People talking, family or friends

You just notice colour,
Gender, sexuality or race

It's always been like that
Well not always
You noticed me but not yourself
You found my love under the shelf
You started to get better
Without a doubt.

Bronte Elena Greta Oliver (12) & Mya
All Saints CE School, Wyke Regis

Snow Time

The snow falls down,
The ground is white like clouds.
The snow on the mountain
Tumbles like an avalanche of anger.
The children play, make snowballs
And build snowmen of joy.
Now the joy has come to an end
And the nature can grow by the snow of winter.

Calvin Hawkins (12)
All Saints CE School, Wyke Regis

Endangered Animals

As I lie here looking up at the sky,
Watching the fluffy clouds go by,
A beautiful snow leopard appears before my eye
And I sit here and wonder, will another die?
With so few of them left in the wild,
Will they still be here when I have a child?

You poached a tiger for a trophy on your wall,
Can you really not see that is so cruel?
Or killed an elephant just for its tusk,
Why do you have to be so brusque?
Gorillas killed for meat or a charm,
But all you do is cause pain and harm.

Please, please put down your gun,
Why do you have to make these animals run?
You do it for fun or just for a game,
But all you do is hurt and maim.

So I beg you, please put down your gun
And leave these animals free to run.

Bethany Gribble (12)
Brannel School, St Stephen

Opinion

It's your opinion
It's not your friend's or your family's
It's your choice, the way your brain works.

Don't change your mind because people don't agree
Just make your decision on who you want to be
People want to think the same
But it always turns out plain.

Some judge you on what you wear
But honestly, you try not to care
They look at you and whisper behind your back
That's when you wonder what you lack.

Pointing, staring, giggling and whispering
Do you need to tell someone? Bullying?
What you wear is part of who you are
Not what they are.

If everyone's the same
It would be them to blame
It's not your fault you're different
No one is flawless or perfect.

No one should wear the same clothes
Or have the same hairstyle or cut
We're not symmetrical
We're a miracle.

We can't have the exact same eyes
Or the exact same voice, scream or cries
It's hard to see everything as it is
Only special and specific people
Can see the true way of the world.

Amy Bristow (13)
Brannel School, St Stephen

The Difference

7am, her alarm goes off
The sunrise is her alarm
Fancy watch or clock
She wakes up and complains about the day
She gets up and deals with it the only way
She does her hair, she does her make-up
She does dishes, she does the washing
She puts on a smile
She picks up her bag and waits for the bus
She picks up her bucket and walks through the fuss
She's in class talking and laughing
She's by the river working hard
Dinner time comes she eats her hot meal
Dinner time comes she's waist high in dirty water
She picks up her bag and waits for the bus
She picks up her bucket with her blistered hands
She's on the bus having a good time
She stumbles miles and miles to her home.

Courtney Hitchens (13)
Brannel School, St Stephen

A Man's Best Friend

Dogs are for life, not for fighting or puppy farming,
Not for abusing or over-breeding.

Dogs like fun, not fighting,
Dogs like to play, not abusing,
Dogs like to be fed, not starved.

Dogs are for life, not for neglecting or starving,
Dogs are for cuddling, playing and being happy.

Dogs like fun, not fighting,
Dogs like to play, not abusing,
Dogs like to be fed, not starved.

The dog isn't vicious, the owner raised it to be,
Dogs are for life and a man's best friend.

Dogs like fun, not fighting,
Dogs like to play, not abusing,
Dogs like to be fed, not starved.

Dogs are for life, not just for Christmas.

Hollie Swallow (13)
Brannel School, St Stephen

Stop Judging

You can't do anything in this society
Without being judged
For who you are,
What you are,
Where you are,
Anything.

You get judged on what you wear,
What you look like,
What colour skin you have,
What weight you are,
What culture you are,
What religion you are,
Anything.

We are all the same,
All human,
All have feelings,
All have beliefs,
But we are all very different too.

Some people are spotty,
More chunky,
More skinny,
More nasty,
More kind,
More money,

But more or less,
We are all human.

Do what you want,
Be who you want,
And just be who you are.

Summer Wade (13)
Brannel School, St Stephen

We Are All People

She's black
He's white
But they're both people
They're both different people
But they're both people
They have different genders
But they're both people
And they should be treated right
They should have equal rights
They should be treated the same as everyone else.

Some people are Christians
Some people are Muslims
Some people don't have a religion
But we're all people
We're all different people
But we should all be treated right
We should all have equal rights
We should all be treated the same
As anything and everyone else is.

Olivia Ralph (13)
Brannel School, St Stephen

Bullying

It's not okay to bully!
Why do you feel it's okay to pick on people?
Is it because they are different to you?
Is it because they believe in something you don't?
Is it because they express themselves differently?

Are you really that low?
Is your life that bad that you feel the need to bully others?
How do you think these victims feel?
Do you not feel good enough about yourself?

Did you know that there are about 4,400
Teen and child deaths per year?
One of those deaths could be because of you.
Do you still think this is okay?
It's not, it's not okay to bully!

Tilly Ashby (13)
Brannel School, St Stephen

Suicide

She was perfect,
But she didn't see that.
She *was* skinny,
But she didn't see that.
She *was* beautiful,
But she didn't see that.
She *was* an amazing friend,
But she didn't see that.
Was.

She was driven to kill herself,
'W****!'
'Kill yourself.'
'Attention seeker!'
'Lose some weight!'

No one realises how much words hurt,
On the inside and out.
Words stay in your thoughts,
Eating you alive.
Scars stay on your skin.
Words hurt.

Alisiana Oliver (13)
Brannel School, St Stephen

An Empty Room

Bullying, why is it a thing?
It's just a saying to hurt someone's feelings.
Bullying is like being locked in a room,
But it's worse than being in an empty room.
You get picked on, punched and thrown to the ground,
Just because you never got to see your dad,
Just because your mother left you.
When you get home, you stand there shattered and in pain,
To see your foster mother turn away.
You can't sleep at night because you cry in pain
Because tomorrow is going to be the same.
Keep your head up and stay alive
Because the life ahead of you is a long drive.

Rhys Vandermerwe (13)
Brannel School, St Stephen

Judgements

Standing outside the gates of Hell,
Where everyone is so judgemental.
You have got to be skinny,
Be pretty and have a nice figure,
They say.

All of this just because
Social media shows these perfect models.
Now everyone wants to be perfect like them.
People are starving, or even self-harming
Just because society makes them feel
Not pretty or good enough.

Really, size or how pretty you are
Doesn't matter.
You are perfect the way you are.
So don't ever change
For the sake of other people.

Chelsi Down (13)
Brannel School, St Stephen

Untitled

The torture I feel,
Just trembles inside.
The fear, the dread,
Fears freeze so many.
Where do they come from?
I know but do I dare tell?

I need to hide inside.
I'm lost, don't know where to go.
My head's lost in a pillow.
I feel like I'm drowning in my head.
It's torture, I can't explain,
This isn't a game.

I want it to fly away,
But one day
It all went over my head.
I felt fine again,
But it's an ongoing thing...

It will come back.

Bradley Way (12)
Brannel School, St Stephen

Rights

Some people say it doesn't matter if you're black or white,
I wonder if this is right?
It was in May he kicked me on that day.
It was in May I fell over and hit the hay,
It was in May, that was the day.
I was on the bus going to give money to the poor,
When a white man kicked me,
I fell off my chair like a tree that had been cut down.
He took my money, why, why, why?
I was bleeding inside and out.
Why are people racist?
Why do people do this?

Danny Oliver (13)
Brannel School, St Stephen

Pick Your Friends Wisely

You don't have a friend who acts sly
You could have a friend who makes you cry with laughter
Have a friend who looks after you.

It's OK to have a different interest
It's OK to have a different dress
It's OK to look like a mess
It's OK to be in a stress.

Don't have a friend who uses you
Don't have a friend who abuses you
Have a friend who amuses you.

Just have a friend who diffuses bad times.

Liam Phillips (13)
Brannel School, St Stephen

People Die In Wars

People die in wars
Which involve religion
Discrimination of all sorts
Like racist names
Discrimination on fames
Is what they call them for no good reason.

People die in wars
Because of colour
We are all the same
We are all human
We are all born for a reason.

People die in wars
For no reason at all
Why don't they ban wars?
Then there will be applause
We are all human
We are all born for a reason.

Aaron Williams (12)
Brannel School, St Stephen

You Don't Have To Be Perfect

You feel ugly
You look beautiful
You feel fat
You look skinny

They call you pretty
You think they're lying
You might be big
You might be small
They see you as perfect

They might be rich
You might be poor
They might love themselves
You might hate yourself
Don't self-pity

You're perfect the way you are
They're jealous of you
Always believe in yourself!

Charleanne Ede (13)
Brannel School, St Stephen

The Mysterious Dog Attack

The dog barks,
The frog croaks,
The man lurks in the shadows.

The dog ready to pounce,
The little girl is frightened,
The man screams.

Then the dog quickly attacks the man,
The little girl runs and is never seen again.
The man is still getting attacked, screaming for help.

A woman appears,
She sees the man dead on the ground.
She starts to cry,
Then says goodbye.

Lauren Williams (13)
Brannel School, St Stephen

It's OK To Be Different!

Everyone has inner beauty
It's OK to be different
Different is fun
Same is boring.

If everyone was the same
We would all
Talk the same
Walk the same
Look the same
Think the same.

There is inner beauty
In everything
From a waving tree
To a tiny pea.

Don't change who you are
Because someone told you to
Do it because
You want to!

Sarah Guy (13)
Brannel School, St Stephen

Eat Me

Here I am waiting,
Waiting for you to eat me,
The burger you ordered at Maccies and didn't eat
Because you were full up on those fries you said were delicious.
You never said that to me,
No,
Not me, the innocent quarter pounder you left on the side from yesterday,
Yesterday, the day you ate those fries and left me,
Me, the burger someone else could have had,
But no, you just left me on the side.

Billy Turpin-Brooks (13)
Brannel School, St Stephen

Personality

Friendship, what does it mean?
Having a friend that's not mean.
Friends are there for you,
Maybe someone you can talk to.

I hate people who are racist,
So some people call them hatist,
Why are people like this?

Some people say it doesn't matter
If you're black or white,
I wonder if that's right?
Some people should just look to the light.

Harry Lewis (13)
Brannel School, St Stephen

In June

It was June when you kicked my thigh,
It was June when you punched my eye.
Soon I was hurt but did not cry.
You chucked me off my seat,
Unfortunately, I did not land on my feet.
I hit the floor with a bang,
A kind lady gave me a hand.
She asked if I was alright,
I said, 'That gave me a fright.'
He's a bully and likes to fight,
But he knows he gives me a fright.

Joshua Osborne (13)
Brannel School, St Stephen

Forever Alone

Nobody wants me
I'm forever lonely
I study hard to get a good job
Hopefully I'll be happy
But for now I'm still lonely.

This girl down the road is so beautiful
But I don't have the guts to ask her out
Soon I might run out of time
And I'll still be lonely.

A heart full of love
Lost forever
While I'm
Forever alone.

Ben Millar (13)
Brannel School, St Stephen

Untitled

Back at the barracks
Speaking to my family
All of a sudden that deafening sound
Siren, siren, siren
Can only mean one thing
Grab our gear, guns and boots
Board the tanks and planes
Dropped into the zone
Watching out for the enemy
Bang, bang, bang
Guns and bombs
Everywhere around
So many fallen
Never coming home
All fighting for honour.

Charlie Rowe (12)
Brannel School, St Stephen

The Rain

As the day goes by,
The rain sighs,
Day and night,
The rain finds no light,
Like the tears in my eyes,
The sky cries.

As a tear falls onto the leaf,
It falls onto the grave reef,
As the rain soaks into the ground,
The sun frowns.

The sun gets its payback
By getting its rain back.
When the wind blows,
It forms a rainbow.

Leah Jean Grist (13)
Brannel School, St Stephen

Music

M akes you want to dance
U kuleles are beautiful instruments
S ongs make everything better
I ntelligent word choices
C rowds of people listening

N o one can hate it
O nly music makes everything
T housands of people enjoying
E veryone dances to it
S inging is amazing.

Jessica Weighill (13)
Brannel School, St Stephen

You

You would look at me and smile,
Your white teeth glowing,
Big, passionate lips,
Red and true.

You would sing your words,
Like a bird,
A hummingbird in fact,
So delicate and small.

The memories of you,
Will always stay with me,
Any day or any time,
Through thick and thin,
With every smile.

Cody Dalby (13)
Brannel School, St Stephen

War

The sound of explosions in the night,
Traumatised by this eerie sight.
The cries of loved ones lost in the dark,
But on this quest I shall embark.
To fight for my country, I will stand,
To hold onto my mother's hand.
But I will never forget these sights,
Even if I try with all my might.

Stewart Bryan Heaton (13)
Brannel School, St Stephen

Equal Rights

Why are we different?
Black and white are just colours
'Don't judge another' says your mother

The men have no time for a newborn
But the women do
It's so unfair

Money! Who cares?
We are all better than money
Rich or poor, we should love us all.

Thomas Follington (13)
Brannel School, St Stephen

On The Farm

On the farm,
Waiting for the alarm,
5:30am signs a wake-up call,
To get up, get dressed
And get outside for the long haul.

As the sun rises up above the rolling hills,
The duck bills speak, *quack, quack*,
In a symphony of vibrato trills.

This amazing place has shown me all its charm
And this place
Is on the farm.

Ben Chick
Clayesmore School, Blandford Forum

Bullies

Bullies are tough
They take your stuff
Pointless
Just like the rest.

Bullies are petrifying
Bullies are lonely
Bullies are dumb
Even though
They make us sad
We don't fall down.

Oi, we think we're tough
Yeah!

Gruesome gangs are coming
For you
Boy!

You stupid boy
You're going to
Cry!
Yeah!

You stupid rats
We take your stuff
We are the cool kids
Yeah!

Dylan Green (12), Reece Dowd (11) & Harvey Levy (11)
Cranbrook Education Campus, Cranbrook

Hackers

Broken banks
Hackers grab
Information
Sneaky cats
Place a virus
Dangerous
Like a dagger
Fake IDs
Secret money
Virtual bullies
Hidden ninjas
Lurking tigers
Scamming
Fighting
You don't know
What we've
Been through!

Corbin (12) & Noah Homewood (12)
Cranbrook Education Campus, Cranbrook

Life And Death Go Hand In Hand

Life is a gift
To many, blessed;
More of a burden to others,
A gift to less.

There was a time
When I once read
The living can never
Be the dead.

A future rich as gold,
Opportunities past the sky.
If not to live is right
Then we've all lived a lie.

The poor, hungry and sick
Have something no one can buy;
That wonderful gift, that soaring blessing
The days we are alive.

The trees are like us - human.
Their beauty lies unknown
But there must always be a painful time
When all of us must go.

Lives like ours are special
We carry things that glow.
In power, strength and beauty,
Giving birth to a home.

Before I leave this aching world
Which we destroy and hold
I beg you all to live your lives
As if never getting old.

Deborah Omolegan-Obe (13)
Fairfield High School, Horfield

The Girl Inside

I don't know how to say this,
How to put it into words...
My inability to be normal
Drags me down like a curse.
I mimic others' actions
In an attempt to fit in,
But if society was a plate
I'd be the discards on the rim.

Simple actions scare me,
Make my hands quake with fear.
Large crowds and misspoken words
Cause my eyes to fill with tears.
My friends will often tell me,
'It's nothing, calm down!'
So I keep my fearful words
And draw a smile to hide my frown.

I know I'm good enough,
But what would others say,
If I had one of my moments
In school one day?
I'm not a bad person,
I should have nothing to hide...
But would people still want to know me
If they saw the girl inside?

Maybe I'm just different,
We all are in a way.
I may not even be
The discards on the plate.
Sometimes I doubt if society is right...
If we want to be accepted,
Why should we have to fight?
To be acknowledged,
Why should we have to fit in?
After all,
No one deserves to be the discards on the rim.

I spent my life being a shadow,
Which blocked out the sun.
It left me worn out and hollowed
Until I found a source of fun.
I used to worry about being judged,
Until I realised;
Maybe I could find someone
Who loved the girl inside...

Maisie Woods
Fairfield High School, Horfield

Watching From The Window Seat

Watching from the window seat
Across the bright blue sea
The water trickling
Onto the golden sand
The red and white picnic rug
Spades spread across the ground
Buckets filled with water
The liquid tipping over
The castle of golden sand
Surrounded by a moat
When watching from the window seat
My heart is filled with hope
Blue eyes shine in the sun
As I run down to the beach
'Cause whenever I feel down
I sit, watching from the window seat.

Bethany Skelton (13)
Hele's School, Plympton

Thoughts On 9/11

Around, all around, the mourners gather.
My dread grows as the stroke of death
Falls against my naked soul.
It mutilates me,
And slowly my blood drips to the swirling dust.
In pain I flee,
While death follows.
Now alone, my fervent plea falls
Upon darkened eyes.
This is my doom,
This is my end,
There's nowhere to go, nowhere to run,
Haunting my every last moment in this so-called luxury.
This is God's choice, His sin.
Now my rotten corpse is fed to the Devil himself.
What have you done to me?
A black cloud of chaos as memories darken,
Once I tasted innocence, wide-eyed and childlike,
But my hope perished.
A sickening vision of lies,
Emotions follow pain, follow hate,
Love left to die
In a haze of bitterness.
I see you no more.
The night falls in a heavy
Suffocating cloak, cold and alone I am.

The light for which I lust flares once then dies.
Swallowed by the all-encompassing dark,
All hope must surely perish.
My heart beats no more
How could you leave me?
Lost souls surround me, crying.
I have fallen,
I jumped.
I stared down at my broken corpse,
Just my soul lived
Until it was to be devoured by the Dark Knight.
Was I just to burn in the flames that surrounded me,
Or to wait until the rubble had crushed my soulless corpse?
I made my choice to jump so that I could see my life flash before my eyes,
To see all the good and bad times
I have shared with the acquaintances around me,
But none of that matters now.
I. Am. Dead.
My body may be gone but my soul lives on and the one thing
I will remember is
September 11th 2001.

Ambher Davy (15)
Hele's School, Plympton

Teenage Friendships - Friends For-Never

Friends forever, you promised.
Never to part, you said.
But now we've fought,
And I'm lying here crying on my bed.

Part of me feels that I'll never be the same,
Sure we've fought before,
But they were always fixed
And we both took responsibility for the problem,
But in this one fight,
You said there was only one person to blame...
Me.

I've always been there for you
And I always will,
Because I cared about you then,
And I care about you still.

Friends forever,
Was what we said we'd always be,
But look what's happened today,
We've fought and now you're gone.
So what I really need you to see,
Is what you made it feel like,
All the tears I've cried,
The hurt I've felt all through the night,

You said friends forever,
But really,
It was friends for-never.

Caitlin Barnes (14)
Hele's School, Plympton

I Hear Him Cry

Each day I watch my grandad walk,
I hear him cry, I hear him talk.
He speaks of loved ones no longer here,
I hear him cry, I see his tears.
Alzheimer's is stealing his life away.
I hear him cry, I fear that day.
He needs help with his daily routine,
I hear him cry, I help him clean.
He can't cut his food - so he can't eat,
I hear him cry, I keep him neat.
He often seems to forget his past,
I hear him cry, I can't let it last.
Frustrated and helpless as the day goes by,
I lost him here, I cleared my eyes.

Each day I watched my grandad walk,
I heard him cry, I heard him talk.
He always struggled, he always tried,
You ask me now, yes... I cried.

Cerys Siobharn Read (14)
Helston Community College, Helston

So Much Right In Wrong

The roof I live under, protects me from thunder
The clothes on my back, stops the cold coming back
The shoes on my feet, no more pain or defeat

My sister and brother, my father and mother
Protect me from harm, and the loud smoke alarm
Protects me from fire, so why do I feel
Like I'm never succeeding, and that this world is so dire?

The tests that I take, a career they will make
The guys that I date, for the right I will wait
The friends that I make, not to last, they are fake

My sister and brother, my father and mother
Protect me from harm, and the loud smoke alarm
Protects me from fire, so why do I feel
Like I'm never succeeding, and that this world is so dire?

The future I create, no denying my fate
The life I will live, soon enough I will give
The children I will birth, so much love and worth

My sister and brother, my father and mother
Protect me from harm, and the loud smoke alarm
Protects me from fire, so why do I feel
Like I'm never succeeding, and that this world is so dire?

Erin-May McMichael (13)
Marine Academy, St Budeaux

Freedom To The King

Hands to the heavens,
No man, no weapons.
Formed against us, glory is destined.
Every day women and men become legends;
Sins that go against our skin become blessings.
The movement is a rhythm to us,
Freedom is like religion to us,
Justice is a juxtaposition in us.
Justice for all: is just not specific enough.
One son died, his spirit was revisiting us,
It was living - living in us.
That's why Rosa sat on a bus;
That's why we walked through Ferguson with our hands up.
When it goes down, woman and man up!
They say stand down; but we stand up
Shots, we're on the ground,
The camera panned up.
King pointed to the mountain top
And we ran up!

Leah Gotham (14)
Marine Academy, St Budeaux

Books

My lives are hidden
Within the books I read
Secrets in my mind
That nobody else knows

People say I'm strange
But I totally agree
I am strange
But there are different perspectives of normal

One could be not like me
Another could be not like them
Another could be completely the same as me
Again everyone's perspective is different

Books open for you to read
They close so you can start another
It's almost like travelling in time and space.

Milly Lecount (13)
Marine Academy, St Budeaux

Love You Mummy

I met a girl,
She was lovely.
She may be ill,
But she was cuddly.
Her name was Tanya,
Described like this:
  T - truthful, would never lie,
  A - angelic, a voice as smooth as an angel,
  N - naughty, always up to mischief,
  Y - young, only 31,
  A - amazing, best mum ever,
Before God took the best,
Gave Mum a rest,
We wrote poems and stories like this.
Let's just say,
Before you fly away,
Love you, Mummy,
Watch over us every day.

Jade Thomas (13)
Marine Academy, St Budeaux

The Lonely Moon

I am a lonely moon
The pale-faced, empty child.
I often ask myself,
Why have I never smiled?

I am a lonely moon,
Abandoned, heartbroken girl.
I often think about,
Who's there on Mother World?

I'm friendless, cold and scared,
Too shy to venture out.
So when the day lights up,
I hide, don't talk or shout.

I am that lonely moon,
The strange, mysterious she.
Alone all day and night,
Even stars stay away from me.

Eloise Beattie (15)
Penryn College, Penryn

Up There

Up there
Sitting in your ray of sunshine
Passionate, loyal, trustworthy.
Every day I come to you,
In content or in doubt,
You always listen.
Up there
My bubble of fear disappears when I hear your voice,
When I need you the most.
You mend my pains and renew me for a new day
You never get bored.
You inspire. You love
Up there
Everywhere
Anywhere
Always
Even when I don't need you
You will wait for my every call
Up there
Waiting...
For me?
In everyone whether they want you or not
Who are you?
Are you even there?
Up there
I hear you call my name

Welcome me into your kingdom;
Of eternal love and joy
Where I will never die
Standing tall at the top of a mountain
Up there
My heart wrenches each time I sin
But I know that you will forever forgive
And forget the bad things I have done
And love me forever
Up there
I know you are listening
To my every word
People say I'm crazy
But my love will always be with you
Forever and ever
Up there
All I have to say is
I love you
I am sorry
But I can't say it to your face
Were you even there at all?

Daisy Booker (15)
Penryn College, Penryn

Donald Trump

Yellow hair,
Orange skin.
He's not fair,
I certainly hate him.

He's a racist bloke,
He's a sexist man.
He is certainly not broke,
He has many thousand grand.

How is he president?
Many people have asked;
To some bad vibes he sent,
Soon he will be unmasked.

Even though he did a TV show;
He's as bad an actor as a hack!
I'm surprised the producer didn't say no;
I could nearly hear Donald say quack.

He's such a hypocrite!
His wife is foreign.
Though to others he will transmit:
Get out of my country, you moron!

Everything about him,
Makes me feel uneasy;
Who'd like a man so grim?
His personality is so sleazy.

(Now read from bottom up)

Lila Mae Sefi (12)
Penryn College, Penryn

Think, Don't Laugh

It's fine to be different;
Some people may be taller than you,
Others may be shorter than you,
You're your own person,
There will be people that are better looking than you,
There will be people that are slimmer than you,
It doesn't matter.

You might look at people and get jealous,
But there will be people looking at you in the same way,
Maybe even the people that you're jealous of may look at you in the same way,
Be happy with who you are,
If you want to be slimmer or a different weight, try to change it,
Don't give up after a few days, keep going.

You may look at someone and laugh at their appearance,
Because they may have different colour skin,
Because they may be bigger than you,
Don't laugh at them,
Because they may be trying to change,
They may want to change,
They may hate themselves because of the way they look,
They may be trying to change.

Would you really laugh at someone
Only because they're different to you?
Think,
They might be hurting themselves because of you,
Because of you blades might be found,
Think,
Fear will look at them in the face like themselves when they look in the mirror,
They try not to look, walking past the shop windows or mirrors,
They won't want to look at themselves because of you,
They'll turn their heads purposely so they don't see their reflection,
Soon they'll hate themselves so much that they'll not want to live anymore,
They'll try to fly but the rope will stop them,
Then that guilt will be on our back for the rest of our lives,
So do everyone a favour and think,
No one likes bullies.

Katie Machin
Redruth School, Redruth

Discrimination

You have no idea how much fear I feel when I'm hated against,
Discriminated against,
I feel afraid,
Alone,
What is it that keeps me going?
I don't know,
But all I show is that you are beating me,
You have defeated me,
But I will not let this beat me,
See, I'm going to stand up for what's right,
The truth is brutal and it is fatal that I should utilise my never-ending cry and say goodbye to you,
'Cause I'm manning up for the fight but I can't, it's not right,
Now go out there and show them tonight,
But that's when you realise that you're not in the right,
You've only sunk to their level,
Might as well meet the Devil,
'Cause now I'm drowning,
This can't be happening,
I think I'm ending,
You're stuck in a never-ending circle,
But I think now it's time to swim up,
That's why I'm writing this song,
I'll let my spirit live on when I'm gone,

Face my fears,
Wipe my tears,
And live on, it's up to you now,
Give an effort, make a difference,
Discrimination never changes,
So, help our nation.

Shaun Thomas Goodman (12)
Redruth School, Redruth

Love Is The Key

L ove is not a lesson you learn, it's a skill.
O nly a few people think it's not true love, they think it's a lesson but it's not.
V iciousness tells others they are not right because of their appearance but it's what's on the inside that counts.
E veryone deserves a chance even though you don't think you're their type but they might be.

I ndividual people have a different boy or girl they dream of.
S ome people don't care if they date someone as long as they're happy.

T ales say that when Cinderella is a slave and then she marries a prince, it's a 0% chance but it might happen.
H appiness is the key to a new relationship that draws boys and girls, men and women together.
E ach person deserves a chance to love and laugh, even if you think and feel it's not right.

K eep one another safe and warm even if you feel you can't keep them for much longer, it still matters.
E ven though they might not be for you, they still matter.
Y oung minds need to grow knowing not everyone falls in love straight away.

Amelia Worden (12)
Redruth School, Redruth

A Better World Through Bombing?

The ominous thought looms over me,
It has me weeping at the knee,
I shed a tear,
Of grief and fear,
For families who have lost someone dear,
I wipe my tired eyes,
And to no surprise,
Another bombing has taken place,
I think it's an absolute disgrace,
We've no idea why,
I feel myself well up, once again about to cry,
They press the trigger and let go,
Then turn it to themselves, press again and stop the blood mid flow,
And why? Well, we just don't know,
Then straight after everyone turns to racism,
But OK, last time I checked we were all the same,
It doesn't matter about from where we came,
Don't turn to hate crime and beatings,
Listen to what the world leaders say after their meetings,
So please, if not for you or I, do it for the next generation,
So they a chance for the world to let them see,
The ominous thought loomed over me,
It has me weeping at the knee.

Jamie Lowenna Collick (12)
Redruth School, Redruth

Terrorism

You stare into the eye of the bomb
You start to flee
The trigger is pressed
Terrorism.

Your house is gone
Your home is gone
Terrorism
Terrorism.

The professionals come
They check for fingers
They track with success
Terrorism.

They find the culprit
They are dead on the floor
They take money to rebuild
Terrorism, terrorism.

You saw people walking outside
As the bomb went off, *boom!*
Their flesh and their bones have been blown to bits
Terrorism.

The army sets off for war
To fight the terrorists
There is still more suffering
Terrorism, terrorism.

They still come back
And bomb some more
Their hearts as cold as the Arctic
Terrorism.

The protestors protest
As the army shoot
The terror is to bomb
There is no end to terrorism.

If you try to stop it you will have the same awful fate
By the terrorism loop of death
Trying to stop it, fail and repeat
Terrorism, terrorism.

Leo Vaughan (12)
Redruth School, Redruth

Emotions

E verybody feels them
M any people ignore them
O nly time will tell
T he feelings you feel
I nside yourself
O ver your strength emotions will win
N ever giving mercy
S table or not, we all feel them

D enial, betrayal, they never seem to fail
O ur faces cover up the true feelings inside
N ever letting them see your weakness
T hey're telling a story that isn't true

H iding your feelings
I do it too
D on't be ashamed
E verybody feels them

Y ou need to embrace
O ur true feelings inside
U nderstood or not
R eveal your inner self

T rust yourself
R egret nothing
U nderstanding or not
E verybody feels them

S ome people
E mbrace their emotions
L eaving hidden feelings forgotten
F orever!

Darcey Christine Jago (12)
Redruth School, Redruth

Anti-Bullying

Freddie is sitting in his locker
Like a lonely hamster in a cage
While James is laughing at him
Eating away at his confidence.

He is crying, thinking, *why?*
Why me?
Meanwhile, James is thinking
Let's kick him one more time.

When Freddie goes home
He cooks for his family
While James is playing on his PlayStation
Waiting to be fed his favourite meal.

At the weekends
Freddie goes to work at his local store
However, James is going to buy
A new phone.

Freddie's school life got so bad
That one night he took a gun
A gun that no 13-year-old should have
He pulled it up to his head and then, *bang!*

James heard about the news
He was devastated because
No matter how hard he tried to deny it
He knew that it was his fault
His fault that a life had been lost.

Rebekah Pearce (13)
Redruth School, Redruth

A Big Bang

A big bang
People screaming
Roof collapsing
It's all happening now
Feeling like I'm constantly falling
My head is pounding
A big bang.

People are trying to help me
But it doesn't matter now
We shall not stand and bow
Police are crowding me
Protecting me
But there is no need now
A big bang.

We have to carry on
We can't let them stop us
We have to be free
Like a bee
But I think it's time to flee
A big bang.

Like a flash
People are ready to dash
Bad boys coming after you
Will you come back?
I have no clue
All we know is about
The children not coming back
A big bang.

How can this happen again?
Again and again
Terror is Hell
They won't stop us
Be strong
Prove them wrong
Tell them you're right
A big bang.

Josh Ebling
Redruth School, Redruth

Unique

Everybody's different,
We are all unique.
Why should we be prejudice about someone who is black or white?
They did not choose,
We are equal,
We all bleed the same,
We all feel happiness, hate and pain,
We are all different,
From tall to short,
To fat to thin,
To gay to straight,
To boy to girl.
We are unique,
We are born originals,
We all make decisions,
We sometimes don't have a voice,
We can't feel happiness without sadness,
Bang! Blood ran down my face,
For what?
For being myself, unique and different.
I got home,
'Well, it is your fault,
You chose to be like this,' said Mum.
So I thought, *did I really choose who I am or was I born this way?*

Think anti-prejudice before you judge,
It's like stabbing someone for who they are.

Madison Symons
Redruth School, Redruth

I Am Fine

I am alive and that is great
I am alive but am I living?
I tell you I am fine
But I go home and cry
I believe telling you will make me seem petty
So I hide
I am fine.

The monsters are believed to be under your bed
But they run amok inside my head
They scream my every thought
Shadows of my self-doubt
Screaming
Fat
Ugly
Stupid
Every day
I am fine.

If you stared into my eyes
You may see me break
Like a ticking time bomb
Just waiting for a slither of hope, love and happiness
Every day

Tick
Tick
Tick
I am fine.

Most days I sit and watch
Everyone seems so well put together
So I put on an act
But when no one is looking
Society's demons attack
I may look perfect
But if you only knew
What a smile can hide
I am fine.

Kalya Christine Manley (13)
Redruth School, Redruth

The Dark Night

The night was dark,
For a guy called Mark,
He walks on,
Thinking the battle is won.

John with a life at stake,
Lifts his head up awake,
He hears a dog bark,
Then he sees Mark.

Mark knocks on John's door,
Soon kicking it to the floor,
John walks out and says, 'Hey, what's going on?'
Mark says, 'Now I have won.'

John stands there poised, still,
Mark sets up for the kill,
John gets shot in the head,
Then falls to the ground, dead.

Mark dashed off steadily,
With the police car at the ready,
He could just make out the sound of wheels,
With the police at his heels.

Kid, you've been caught,
Because of all of those you have fought,
I am going to put you in prison,
For all you have imprisoned in death.

Adam Richards (12)
Redruth School, Redruth

A Man's Best Friend

I remember I wanted to go to the beach,
All it took was to say the words, 'Let's go,'
My dogs hopped up and jumped around,
As we popped into the car as fast as we could.

When we arrived, all was good,
The sun was out,
And the water was cool,
Their tails were wagging as quick as a flash,
As they jumped out the car,
They ran as fast as they could,
And sniffed other dogs.

We set up our little tent,
And ate our lunch,
I took my dogs and explored some caves,
Then we went into the sea,
And splashed about,
Splish, splash,
To stop us from getting too hot.

We sat back into our little pink tent,
And our ice creams in hand,
And we watched the sun set,
I think that dogs are the perfect pets,
And will forever be man's best friend.

Kimberley Thomas (13)
Redruth School, Redruth

Love, Affection, Passion

Love, affection, passion,
Is she attractive or is she not?
Tenderness, fondness, keenness,
The love between Romeo and Juliet.
The ode, does he love me or does he not,
Shall we kiss, shall we hold hands or what?
The single people lie in bed,
While the other lovers are going out instead.
Hopelessly devoted and a bunch of love songs,
If you don't have a lover then they sound wrong.
But soon they sound sweet and warm,
That's only when you find a lover to hold.
It's when they finally let go it feels so bad,
It's when you realise what you had.
Your boyfriend, your girlfriend, your sweetheart,
I'm just playing my part.
You can love when you're old, you can love when you're young,
Love songs are the only thing we ever sung.
Love, affection, passion.

Maisie Cornish (12)
Redruth School, Redruth

No One

Sometimes a man gets carried away
When he feels like he should play
And much too blind he is to see the damage he has done
Sometimes a man has to awake to find he has no one.

He wakes to see no one by his side
He wakes to find he has to cry
He gets dressed and runs out the door
Screaming, 'I don't want to live anymore.'

He gets in his car
But feels so far
From his life of which he came
As all he does is ever blame
On his luck
He feels as if he is some muck
Just tucked away
From the day
Forever night
He can't fight.

He misses her
He hears a purr
Of the traffic
All her stuff is in the attic
He tells himself she'll come back
But his knowledge seems to lack
As she is never coming back.

Tom Clarke Sharples (12)
Redruth School, Redruth

Love - The Power Of Love

It may not be for you,
But remembering it could help you through,
Hard and sad times,
Love has lots of power,
Helping you through sadness,
Helping prevent madness.

Love can be shared,
Love shouldn't be scared,
Life is made of love,
Flying around like a flock of white doves.

Celebrating love makes people happy,
Leaving love can make people down,
But recalling love always removes frowns,
From faces all around.

Love can help you win,
And remove and forget all sins,
Love is life,
Removing all the fright,
From conflict and war,
Everyone should have more,
Have more love,
Love swallows us.

To live a happy life,
Don't forget the doves,
The symbol of a power,
The power known as love.

Lilli Wright
Redruth School, Redruth

I Remember

I remember
When life was fun
Exciting and full of surprises
I remember
When we couldn't
Stop smiling
We were always happy
I was younger then
Suddenly, all fun stopped
Because of him
I was just a child
I didn't understand
I remember
You came home with bruises
Cuts and tears on your face
Asked what was wrong
You said it was 'nothing'
And went to your room
We stopped playing
You said it hurt to move
But Mum knew
It was him, not you
Mum spoke to him one night
She asked him to leave
But he wanted to fight
He pulled out a gun and shot

Bang! Bang!
I couldn't understand
After that you disappeared
Do you remember?

I do...

Deanna Watson (13)
Redruth School, Redruth

The Innocent Beach

Many tourists lie on the golden sands,
With suncream and flip-flops in their hands.
Seagulls squawk impatiently over their heads,
As seaweed and sharp rocks attack the seabed.

The whispering ocean ushers me in,
And soon enough, I am lost within.
A tangle of hair, saltwater and more,
As the strong rip current thrashes me to the floor.

I scream and scream but nothing comes out,
I'm hopeless till I hear a distant shout.
The voice sounds panicked and slightly hoarse,
Then it hits me, it's the lifeguard of course!

Two strong hands grab me from the sea,
But no cough or splutter escapes from me.
He pumps my chest on the edge of the seabed,
It's a shame I can't tell them, I'm already dead.

Holly Thompson (12)
Redruth School, Redruth

Rugby

Rugby is a quick game
But if you lose there is no shame
You can play it with your mates
Just make sure you have a certain date
It's always fun.

Make sure you start with touch
Because you don't want to get hurt too much
And if you think that you're the best
Then we will put you to the test
It's always fun.

If the other team score a try
Just make sure you don't cry
As it's always fun.

If you're kicking the ball
Make sure you don't fall
As it's only fun.

When you finally win a game
Make sure you all get the fame
So, when you're celebrating
Make sure the other tea aren't hurting
Because rugby is always fun.

Samuel Linthwaite (13)
Redruth School, Redruth

World War

I'm seeing the poor suffer in the world war
They didn't get evacuated
Because they had no family members
To evacuate them and say bye
Their lives are in danger
They are left to starve
They have bad lives
World war.

The world war is cruel
To people who are poor
War
The poor suffer
The war should stop
The war should not be beating the poor.

The poor are homeless
The poor are starving
The poor are cold
The poor are thirsty
The war should stop.

The war
The war
The war should not be here
The war is cruel
The war is a killer.

People with homes are gone
Their homes are gone
The war should have died
It should not have been alive.

Jessica Reynolds (12)
Redruth School, Redruth

Humanity

The trees blow
Flowers grow
The birds tweet
In celebration of peace.

Before the grass comes down
And the concrete is all around
The animals cry
As the trees all die
Is this nature's goodbye?

Now you can see just gravel
As the humans unravel
The blanket of nature
It won't be there later
Just piles of paper.

While species are driven to extinction
The trees say, 'Are the people even thinking?'
Their peacekeeping efforts are in vain
The humans will just cause the pain.

Now the smoke is in the air
And animals have no hair
The forest is at a halt
Humans, this is your fault!
All this to satisfy your desire.

Jake Neville (12)
Redruth School, Redruth

Scared And Lonely

I was scared and lonely all by myself,
I didn't know if I was going to die or not.
I was full of fear, it was the end of the year.
Some came near my side, near the great ocean tide looking at the sky.
I hear a deer that was crying a single tear.
I was walking towards a girl,
Her eyes were shiny like a pearl.
The girl was full of fear, I could barely hear her.
I asked her to speak up but I still couldn't hear her.
All I could hear was the ocean wave, a seal jumped up called Dave.
We lay on the cooling sand, the girl held my hand.
She held my hand like we were in a band together.
She looked at me like I hooked something.
She lay next to me like I was a piece of hay.

Caitlin Kira Roberts (14)
Redruth School, Redruth

Think

I go to school,
Dreading the day ahead,
I just want my bed,
They think they can be missed,
But they're just prejudice.

I don't want to leave home,
So I pretend I'm ill,
But that's kinda dull,
Don't want to tell family or friends,
But that's if I had some,
So they're just prejudice.

You don't even think,
You're like a tiger hunting prey,
Why do you bother?
Back to my own country,
This is,
So you're just prejudice.

Why do you do it?
What do you gain?
It just puts us in pain,
All these words you say,
Because you're just prejudice.

Ben Grimsted
Redruth School, Redruth

Mi Abuela

You wake up and she isn't there,
Nothing but a single hair,
The person you need the most,
Is now just a ghost.

Illnesses took her away,
Now all you do is pray,
Hoping she is safe,
Now she's in a better place.

It's been a week now,
All you wear is a frown,
All you wanted is for her to stay,
But she was taken away.

Do you love someone?
Do they like to have fun?
Do you love someone?
Do they like to have fun?

Do they share memories with you?
Do they know when it's their cue?
Do they take you on fun days?
Do they take you out in the rain?

Molly-Victoria Harris (12)
Redruth School, Redruth

Stumbled Stag

As I got my rifle I finished my bowl of trifle
Then I got my sack and my hat
Then I got a call
From the Wild Welfare Trust
About a stumbled stag
I got my shotgun shells
Made my way over to the destination
As I arrived, there was the stumbled stag
I got into position
Cocked my gun until it sprung,
Loaded a bullet into the thick barrel
As I lined him up in my sights
He called out, then I knew
The stumbled stag had to go
I put the safety off
Finger on the trigger
Ready to kill the big, black figure,
As I shot the big, black figure
He stopped and dropped to the ground
Without fear!

Harley Matthews (14)
Redruth School, Redruth

Life Is Crying

L ife is luxury, life is loving.
I t isn't how it seems, it is just how it seems to you.
F ighting, hurting, killing as words stab you like knives.
E very day living people start lying there
  crying, surrounded by dying.

I t has now been realised, those hidden secrets.
S cared nights, not a happy mite.

C hildren's lives filled with fright.
R unning away into the cold night.
Y ou feel a sense of spite.
I n the end it all works out.
N othing will stop you.
G o tell yourself that you are strong then move on.

Eleanor Dennis (12)
Redruth School, Redruth

This Society

Why do we hate on others?
This society is messed up,
Hating on people because of their race and skin colour,
Hating them just because they don't look like you,
That's just messed up.

Why do we want to kill each other?
This society is messed up,
Bombs blow up, like volcanoes erupt,
Killing children,
Destroying families,
That's just messed up.

Why do people care what others look like?
This society is messed up,
We body shame people,
Call them fat, fat, fat,
People wear make-up,
So we call them fake,
That's just messed up.

Kacey Barber (13)
Redruth School, Redruth

One Huge Bang!

One huge bang
People screaming
Shouting, running.

Sirens buzzing, police are here
Shouting, 'Get home sweet home.'
But I can't leave, have to find Mum
I hear people shouting
Dead, dead! People are dead!

I start running, crying
My favourite night gone
22 lives lost, I hear someone calling
With a cracked voice like glass.

It's Mum's spirit
I hear calling for me
Telling me to say goodbye to Dad from her.

One, two, three, one loud bang
Silence is gone
22 lives lost forever.

Emily Jose (12)
Redruth School, Redruth

The Touch Of Death

He lay his cold fingers on my tear-stained cheek,
As children around me lay looking bleak.
Mother was crying, Father on his knees,
Please make him better, please, please!

He's the light of my life,
The salt to my sea.
He is the air to my lungs,
And makes me happy as can be.

Why has such a curse bestowed upon him?
I should take his place, be torn limb from limb.
As long as he lives to see another day,
I shall be happy no other way!

The room was silent as the dead of night,
His breathing stopped, he had lost his fight!

India Bennett-O'Brien
Redruth School, Redruth

Environment

E is for the ecosystem and how it holds us together.
N is for nature and nature's forever.
V is for vegetables that keep us strong.
I is for insects that may look wrong.
R is for reptiles that run quickly.
O is for octopuses that look quite sickly.
N is for nutrients that the plants suck up.
M is for the mane that grows on a lion pup.
E is for the environment that surrounds everything.
N is for nectarines that leave us with a zing.
T is for thanking nature for everything that it brings.

Billy Packenas (13)
Redruth School, Redruth

The Great Terror

As the evening clears
Thousands of fans full of cheers
As the song comes to a close
No one knows.

A man like any other
Makes a grave mistake
Without any choice
A flame on a fuse he creates.

As smoke fills the corridors
Orange flames explode the mass of tunnels
The blast sends him flying
Destroying the many doors.

As the terror attempts to rip the city apart
The people of Manchester unite
All they want to do is fight
The great terror as one
Even though they are full of fright.

James Glasspool
Redruth School, Redruth

Battlefield

I arrived on the battlefield,
There were bombs, people dying everywhere,
Soldiers getting hit and blown to bits,
Everyone around me is dying, they need to just save me from lying.

British soldiers are guaranteed to be the best,
Apart from when the Americans came from the West,
German generals have all the power,
Not now when I knock them down tower to tower.

Reloading my gun was the right thing to do,
Now I need to save the Jews,
All everyone is doing is groaning,
I tell them to shut up and stop moaning.

Curtis Holland (14)
Redruth School, Redruth

Kings

Cold was the night as the leaves take flight,
boarding the wind to turn off the light.
As the trees get undressed,
the flowers are depressed and droop down,
Scared of the night ahead.

The sun falls down into the abyss of the night,
and the moon climbs into the sky.
Now winter is king, as the wind kills.

In the dead of night -
arises a spark of light,
illuminating the destruction of winter.
As God hits rewind, the cold is left behind,
the moon rolls back to its den.
Now spring is king.

Louie Fowler-Beaton
Redruth School, Redruth

Why War?

War,
Why war?
Just because you hate someone,
And they hate you back, doesn't mean war,
War makes innocent people die,
Because they are against you,
The innocent don't have a weapon,
But you still kill them,
You're using the soldiers' lives like money,
As the family cry,
You don't care and just say bye-bye,
There are no winners in war,
Just losers,
What did WWI do?
WWII, Vietnam and both Gulf wars?
Nothing!
So, listen up and don't start a war!

Joshua Weller (13)
Redruth School, Redruth

Mother Nature

As the emerald-fresh leaves fall,
which hits the red brick wall.
Silently, small trees sway
like rippling waves.
Small blackbirds sing,
with their delicate wings.
Quickly, an explosion of unwanted trash,
which rapidly attacks,
an animal's habitat
Loudly, the robins squeal, shriek and shudder,
with plastic stuck through its beak.
It slowly becomes very weak.
Why let animals suffer pain?
When you can stop this.
Give dropping litter a miss
help out animals by doing this.

Tara Charlotte Bawden (12)
Redruth School, Redruth

Strong

When a leaf drops
From a family tree
A tear drops
From an eye

But stay strong
Because you have done nothing wrong

When your friend
Ditches you
For another friend
It makes you want to cry

But stay strong
Because you have done nothing wrong

If you drop your books
And everyone looks
Someone will have the guts
To help you pick up your books

But stay strong
Because you have done nothing wrong.

Lilly-Rose Kelly Stannard (12)
Redruth School, Redruth

Attack

Looking around the death-stricken place
People stumbling ready to race
Everyone dashing around and around
Like they're going on a merry-go-round.

Ear-splitting bangs filled your ears
As everyone stood there in fear
Sirens screeching, getting closer
As everyone runs towards safety.

One by one people stumble out
Everyone shouts for their life
Praying their family is OK
Silence filled everyone's breath
All around is silence still.

Caitlyn Harris
Redruth School, Redruth

Precursors

They're all gone...
In one second, wiped out,
From our tyrannosaurus rex
And the infuriating Ceratosaurus, gone.
No wait for it to hit, just gone in the blink of an eye,
A meteor on a genocide of dinosaurs,
The biggest reptiles in history,
Gone with our world,
Even in its worst condition it came back to life,
Plants grew, flowers blossomed and our ancestors gone,
Bones being the only trace of our precursors,
The Earth was repopulated.

Lucy Gemma Hulme (14)
Redruth School, Redruth

Death In The Air

The death... the death deceives the deadly night,
And gives a random family a fright,
A member falls asleep forever,
One day, we will be together,
The tears of sadness start to appear,
With everybody around here,
On their knees, silently screaming to the sky,
Saying to their relative, 'Goodbye!'
There's nothing you can do right now,
Except from have a cry,
For God that person in the sky,
Is looking after your dead ones.

Alfie Jack Rahn (11)
Redruth School, Redruth

Perfect Women

Society, not a nice place to be,
Especially when magazines are showing me,
Showing me how to live my life,
Why can't I be free?

Skinny models on the front page,
Looking slender, unhealthy and beautiful,
Making unrealistic expectations,
Why can't I be free?

Why can't I be toned, thin, thigh gap?
To not feel fat when I eat a bacon bap,
They all have spindly legs,
Do I want mine looking like pegs?

Mia Jose (13)
Redruth School, Redruth

Friends

Friends are here for us,
Friends believe in us,
Friends shouldn't bring you down,
Down, down to the ground,
Friends aren't just at school,
You can meet friends at the mall,
But when you lose a friend,
It makes you feel like the world is going to end,
But in the end you get a friend again,
And that friend could be called Ben,
Everybody needs a friend,
Then you can go to the shop and take some money to spend.

Gemma Richards
Redruth School, Redruth

How The World Changes

People bleeding, people running,
People screaming, people dying,
I'm just watching, I'm just staring,
I don't believe that my eye is daring.

To see this pain and suffering,
I just hope that this can stop in the next 24 hours,
So that this world can improve to be
A non-racist world.

Hopefully in the future,
This can finally stop,
A world without racism,
Is what we all deserve.

Connor Taplin (12)
Redruth School, Redruth

My Thoughts

Sometimes people are bad,
Which forces me to be depressed or mad.
I try to express my feelings in writing,
But the sadness and anger I'm always fighting.
If I was turned into weather it would be rain,
Even though I seem in pain.
I'm happy most of the week,
Some people try and be funny,
Attention they are trying to seek.
Little do they know,
I'm hurt inside,
But it doesn't show.

Sophie Eddy (11)
Redruth School, Redruth

Weather

It's the weather,
The gusts of wind blow through the heather.

Rain floods roads and waters plants,
But it does kill a lot of ants.

Bad weather, like tornadoes, storm across the land,
But people cry when loved ones die.

Wind makes trees fall over,
Just like when grass goes through a lawnmower.

The wind dances like dancers as it blows about.

Kai Jenkin (12)
Redruth School, Redruth

911 - Scarred

Steve was walking to work on one sunny day
He was hoping the day
Was going to go his way.

He arrived at the Twin Towers
And the sun looked
As big as a flower.

The man called Jim
Was next to him
And Steve said, 'Alright Jim.'

The plane came in
The man called Steve said, 'Watch out, Jim!'
Steve died but Jim was alive.

Lewis Thomas (13)
Redruth School, Redruth

Dear World

I feel so alone,
As if I'm on my own,
My parents won't let me back home,
I want to give up.

People hate me,
I have no safety,
No one will help me,
I want to give up.

While the air fills my lungs,
I just want a shoulder to lean on,
I want to give up.

But I still have hope,
I will cope,
I won't give up.

Shania Medlyn
Redruth School, Redruth

Terror Attack

Ear-splitting bangs and booms.
People running around.
Like they're at a fairground.
Why, oh why?
Guns firing.
People crying.
People running for their life.
Terrorists running with their knife.
Why, oh why?
People running.
The bomb has been dropped ringing in my ears.
People shedding their tears.
Why, oh why?

Thomas Lee Hocking (12)
Redruth School, Redruth

Love And Death

Love and death score the skies,
Whilst you love, you will die,
When you die, you'll go up high,
Rest in peace says love's first kiss,
You are depressed because of love,
Just want life to be like a dove,
But it isn't and you know it,
So you've cut yourself and shown your hate,
Love may be just too late.

Rozie Hamilton (12)
Redruth School, Redruth

Nature

N ature makes the world
A mazing little creatures
T alking to each other about what we do not know
U niverse of nature
R eading it from books
E xpecting it to be perfect and it is.

Trinity Sinkins (12)
Redruth School, Redruth

This Is Why I'm Afraid

You say you love water, but now you stay
inside when it rains.
You say you love the
light but now you always stand in the deep
dark, dappled shade.
You say you love fresh
air, but now you put on a jumper when the
wind blows.
This is why I'm afraid, you'll
say you love me too.

Sinead Taylor (12)
Sidmouth College, Sidmouth

A Feeling He Can't Escape

He felt so alone,
Even though he was surrounded by people,
He felt so cold,
Even though it was warm,
He felt so worthless,
Even though everyone cared about him.

He constantly feels like he's in a box,
Separated from the real world,
Separated from reality,
Separated from everyone.

He can't escape the feeling,
The feeling of being alone,
The feeling of being cold,
The feeling of being worthless,
The feeling of being separated.

The world felt empty, cold,
It felt like a room,
A dark room,
With no windows and no doors,
And he was all alone in that room.

Edie Mai Spooner (12)
Stoke Damerel Community College, Stoke

Baby

I always wished my sister would have a baby,
Despite the nine-month wait,
I tried to persuade her from no to maybe,
But it was no debate.

When I found out,
I shed a tear of joy,
I got up and happily danced about,
My first question was whether it was a girl or a boy?

The wait has been exciting,
My sister has grown and grown,
She's started having tightenings,
I'm not looking forward to the baby's cries and moans.

Soon I'll see the baby,
After the nine-month wait,
My sister was persuaded from no to maybe,
I'll be an auntie, it's no debate.

Natalie Maynard (11)
Stoke Damerel Community College, Stoke

Equal

Everyone should be treated equally,
Everyone should be treated fair,
Everyone should be happy,
Everyone should be treated with care.

Everyone is different,
Yet should be treated the same,
Everyone should be happy,
Because life is like a game.

Everyone might wear similar things,
But they all have a different style,
Everyone likes different things,
So you can't put people into different piles.

Everyone should be treated equally,
Everyone should be treated fair,
Everyone should be happy,
Everyone should be treated with care.

Israel Bond (12)
Stoke Damerel Community College, Stoke

Why Do People Bully?

Why do people bully?
Maybe because they think it's funny,
Or they are just being pure silly.

Why do people bully?
Maybe they are bored of being normal,
Or they just want to set themselves a reputation.

Why do people bully?
It's not nice,
It is cruel.

So, why do people bully?
But to answer that question,
You'd better go ask a bully!

Shania Scott (12)
Stoke Damerel Community College, Stoke

For What Was Left For Me?

A tear seeped out,
Of the corner of my eye.
Reflecting the dazzling light,
Like a diamond.
Mocking my woe,
Mocking my fear.
But I felt no disgrace,
No shame that I was weeping,
For I only felt pain.

My hope,
Lay limp at my side.
A shadow of its former self,
Was caged by my mind.
For joy and happiness had fled me,
Along with my family and burned future.
Leaving me to live,
Unfortunately.

Fire had screamed and savaged lives,
Guns had roared in unimaginable hatred.
It had been chaos - a surge of screaming people,
Trampling each other; nothing mattered anymore,
Everyone for themselves.
And so, I sit here and wallow in anguish,
Wishing that I had gone too!

Joe Dix (13)
Tavistock College, Tavistock

Human Kindness

Would you drive on by a car crash
Or stop and help?
Would you walk to the other side of the road
Or help the person up?

You could lend a hand
To the people in need
You could hold a hand
To help them feel calm.

Speak softly
'You'll be okay,'
Smile reassuringly
Someone is on their way.

Remain steady
Stay calm
Help came
But I will remain.

Douglas Radcliffe
Tavistock College, Tavistock

My Poem

Roses are red
Violets are blue
That's what they say but it just isn't true
'Cause roses are red and apples are too
But violets are violet, violets aren't blue
An orange is orange
But a Greenland isn't green
And a pinkie isn't pink so what does it mean
To call something blue when it's not?
We defile it
But ah, what the heck, it's hard to rhyme violet!

Will Greep (14)
Tavistock College, Tavistock

Expectations

Expectations are the target in front of me,
Expectations,
Expectations are high,
Long, dark night and the target's in front of me,
Expectations are high,
Long, sleepless night and the target's in front of me,
Expectations are high.
I pick up the bow,
Arrow is drawn,
I shoot too low,
My dreams are torn.
Expectations,
Expectations are high,
I miss my mark,
Nowhere to hide,
I am in the dark,
I shouldn't have tried.
Expectations are high,
Then there is light,
The angel with my hand,
We take off in flight,
To a new land,
Expectations are high.

Levi Farrow (14)
The Ridgeway School & Sixth Form College, Wroughton

Poetry

And the haikus ahead are the prosper in front of me
Poems
Poems
Oh, poetry
Poems
Oh, poetry
Five seven fives are the longing inside of me
Poems
Oh, poetry
Simile
And the poem is ready
Simile
And the sounds still steady
Poems
Oh, poetry
The poems get dark, the words are surrounding me
My poems get dark, the silence is over me
Poems
Oh, poetry
One metaphor
For something to savour
Two metaphors
Just to add some flavour
Poems
Oh, poetry
Add jumbled-up words

And the poem is gliding
A random action
And the critics are hiding
Poems
Oh, poetry
The same action again
With a new preposition
Then add a teensy, tiny, little bit of repetition
One
Two
Three
And the poem is boring me
Poems
Oh, poetry
Poem is lighter
My mother is praising me
Poem is light
And a little bit of irony
Four
Five
Six
And the music is saving me
Seven
Nine
Eight
Into the burning ground.

Hollie Zaccaro (14)
The Ridgeway School & Sixth Form College, Wroughton

Perform

And the stage is the music in front of me
Perform
Perform
Perform like me
And the music and drama is swelling inside of me
Perform
Perform like me
Handclap sound
And the steady stage thud
Handclap sound
And the steady stage thud
Perform
Perform like me
Perform
Perform like me
Long, dark nights and the sorrow's in front of me
Long, dark nights and the talent's escaping me
Perform
Perform like me
The strain is the slap
And it stings with the worry
The strain is the slap
And it stings with the worry
Perform
Perform like me
A voice strain shot

The music is the bullet inside of me
Heart scrunched small
And the heartbreak is hiding me
Perform
Perform like me
Heart scrunched small
And the heartbreak is hiding me
Gone
Gone
Gone
And the talent is flooding me
Down
Down
Down
And the talent is leaving me
Cold
Quick
Breath
In the dark, dark night.

Eleanor Woods (14)
The Ridgeway School & Sixth Form College, Wroughton

Seasons

Scarves put away
Sunglasses come out
The start of a new day
The frost hurries out
Springtime
Spring is around
Springtime
Spring is around
Earth turns now
Changes are happening
Springtime
Spring is around
Hot
Fresh
Free
Happiness beams down on me
Memories are made
Suntan is clinging to me
Summertime
Summer is now
Summertime
Summer is now
From green to brown
Leaves are ageing
Ablaze with colour
And snow on the mountains

Autumn
Autumn has grounded
Autumn
Autumn has grounded
Rake
Pile
Leap
Autumn has grounded
Cool, brisk winds
Skeletons of once-full trees
A season of welcoming
Winter
Winter is here with me
Winter
Winter is here with me
Dark nights ahead
Hot chocolates by the fire
Cosy
Bleak
Chill
Ice on the water
Winter
Winter is here with me
Spring comes back around
Seasons change
And so do we.

Lucy Cowell (14)
The Ridgeway School & Sixth Form College, Wroughton

We All Belong To One Human Race

The black people and white people
The young and the old
The weight and the heights
What matters, we're all humans.

We talk differently
We behave differently
We look different
But we don't realise
Within, we're all hurting each other.

I am black, so I must be useless
I am white, so I must be outstanding
Just because we're different colours
Doesn't mean we should be judged.

Some are hated
And some are loved
This is madness
'Cause we should all be loved.

Sometimes we may be rude
Sometimes we may be careless
But just imagine the world
If racism never existed.

The word racism is a powerful word
Which makes the world a violent place
If only there is a way to stop racism
Just think about it
Let's make the world a better place, for every race.

Patricia Caroline Carvalho (13)
The Ridgeway School & Sixth Form College, Wroughton

The Black Woman

Light-filled, her skin glows
They made fun of her prominent nose
Societal and feminine laws she carried on her back
50 fruitful years, her youth doesn't crack.

Oh, black woman
Oh, black woman
How precious you are
Oh, black woman
Morphed herself from beautiful scars.

She will come in undertones
Brown, blue or yellow
A form of her roots is her hair
Which were once eradicated
Kinky, entwined and mellow
Her culture
Continuously appropriated
Authentic souls deteriorated.

Oh, black woman
Oh, black woman
How precious you are
Oh, black woman
Morphed herself from beautiful scars.

The kitchen in her home emits booming aromas of different dishes
The seasoning and flavour like morning kisses
Passionate rhythm she will stir
For God instilled music in her
Black women
Mothers of Earth.

Faith Enotse Ukpoju (14)
The Ridgeway School & Sixth Form College, Wroughton

Depression

My loneliness is the depression in front of me
Alone
Alone like me
Alone
Alone like me
Long, boring days are the nothing in front of me
Alone
Alone like me
Alone
Alone like me
And imaginary friends are the silence in front of me
Alone
Alone like me
Alone
Alone like me
Abusive family are the bruises all over me
Alone
Alone like me
Alone
Alone like me
And my phone is life surrounding me
Alone
Alone like me
Alone
Alone like me
And new, kind voices are starting to reach me

Alone
Alone like me
Alone
Alone like me
And conversation is staring to brighten me
Great new friends are starting to engulf me
And I take a new step into a bright, new life.

Tom Bryan Stokes (14)
The Ridgeway School & Sixth Form College, Wroughton

Sadness

My tears are the flow of life for me,
Sadness,
Sadness,
Sadness fills me,
Sadness,
Sadness fills me,
Late, lonely nights as my tears drown me,
Sadness,
Sadness fills me,
Cry of night,
And I'm on my knees,
Crying my heart is hurting me,
Sadness,
Sadness fills me,
Smile though the day,
Wash the pain away,
Sadness,
Sadness fills me,
My heart breaks,
My mind gets fuzzy,
My heart breaks,
My mind gets fuzzy,
Sadness,
Sadness fills me,
Cry, hurt, shake,
The pain fulfils me,

I hide behind a mask,
But my sadness fights to be free,
Sadness,
Sadness fills me,
Life gets harder,
Days get shorter,
Like my life is taken from me...

Shannon Louise Wolton (14)
The Ridgeway School & Sixth Form College, Wroughton

The Abyss

The darkness
Darkness surrounding me
Lost in the abyss
Shine the light for me
Help me, please
Help me.

Show me the path
Show me the path
Out of this darkness
All alone in the abyss
Help me, please
Help me.

Losing myself in the dark
Alone in the abyss
No path in front of me
Don't know where I'm going
Help me, please
Help me.

It feels like I'm in hell
No one cares
Eyes now surround me
But none of them come to aid, so
Help me, please
Help me.

Reality floods my mind
Crashing down
Crashing down on me
Feeling nothing, too late to
Help me out of the abyss.

George Tweedale (14)
The Ridgeway School & Sixth Form College, Wroughton

YOUNG WRITERS INFORMATION

We hope you have enjoyed reading this book – and that you will continue to in the coming years.

If you're a young adult who enjoys reading and creative writing, or the parent of an enthusiastic poet or story writer, do visit our website **www.youngwriters.co.uk**. Here you will find free competitions, workshops and games, as well as recommended reads, a poetry glossary and our blog.

If you would like to order further copies of this book, or any of our other titles, then please give us a call or visit **www.youngwriters.co.uk**.

Young Writers
Remus House
Coltsfoot Drive
Peterborough
PE2 9BF
(01733) 890066
info@youngwriters.co.uk